THE CELL

THE CELL

Lyn Hejinian

SUN &
MOON

CLASSICS
21

PS
3558
E4735
.C4
1992

Sun & Moon Press
A Program of
The Contemporary Arts Educational Project, Inc.
a non-profit corporation
6148 Wilshire Boulevard, Los Angeles, California 90048

First published in paperback in 1992 by Sun & Moon Press

10 9 8 7 6 5 4 3 2
FIRST EDITION

The passage quoted in the poem of May 22, 1988 is from Henry David
Thoreau's *Ktaadn*.

This book was made possible, in part, through a grant from the Cultural Affairs
Department, City of Los Angeles, and through contributions to The Contemporary Arts Educational Project, Inc., a non-profit corporation.

Some sections of this work have previously appeared in these magazines: *Avec*,
Caliban, *Everyday Life*, *Ironwood*, *Jimmy's and Lucy's House of K*, *Motel*, *Moving
Letters*, *Paper Air*, *O-blek*, *Occident*, *Sequoia*, *Sink*, *Sonora Review*, *Tyuonyi*, and
Writing. The author wishes to thank the editors of these publications. An edition
of twelve of these poems, published in conjunction with twelve poems by Kit
Robinson, was published as *Individuals* (Tucson, Arizona: Chax Press, 1988).

The author would also like to thank the Banff Centre in Alberta, Canada, and
its Leighton Artist Colony, which provided the time and place for completion of
this work.

Cover: *Taking in the Rye*, by Kazimir Malevich
Reproduced by permission of the Stedelijk Museum, Amsterdam

LIBRARY OF CONGRESS CATALOGING IN PUBLICATION DATA
Hejinian, Lyn (1941)
The Cell
p. cm — (Sun & Moon Classics: 21)
ISBN: 1-55713-021-3
I. Title. II. Series.
811'.54—dc19
CIP 90-50335

for Kit Robinson

in correspondence

It is the writer's object
        to supply the hollow green
        and yellow life of the
        human I
It rains with rains supplied
        before I learned to type
        along the sides who when
        asked what we have in
        common with nature replied opportunity
        and size
Readers of the practical help
They then reside
And resistance is accurate— it
        rocks and rides the momentum
Words are emitted by the
        rocks to the eye
Motes, parts, genders, sights collide
There are concavities
It is not imperfect to
        have died

October 6, 1986

There are boulders allowed among
        the cows
Clouds under the thought that
        proved to be too short
Just as one rests an
        hypotenuse there is the feeling
        of hopelessness
The line is not continuous
A stroke in sight and
        blinking
Scale, scale, and flower
In theory there's observation or
        there's prediction to justify
Specificity scooping under the trees
        and red spots immediately absorbed
As well as skeletons cooling
Between mutually exclusive descriptions but
        with difficulty a person might
        decide
So many persons, who cannot
        greet
The sentence is complete and
        separate like a hedgehog, like
        a charcoal, or a rock
The soft world is between
        rocks
The person of which I
        speak is between clocks

October 8, 1986

Exploration takes extra words
Words qua sentience and thinking
These are spread over a
         position— being long and pointed
         over
They anticipate an immoderate time
         and place
Reality moves around making objects
         appear as if they belong
         where they are
Then it shifts, say, up
         and down, with the sunlight's
         yellow interstitial coloring matter
The sun here is an
         exceeding stricture
I've yet ... I keep thinking ...
         all open daylit areas carry
         to peripheries their yellow floating
         ovoid motes
Eggs go out of optical
         range, but only ellipsing
The particular attraction empties in
Blown convincing field, it rattles
         with brown grass turning
I'm looking, prematurely, for a
         particular point of view— that
         of one who has already
         achieved objectivity

Objectivities and metonymies
But one can't die
Sex sexes scale and flies
        faithful to the ground

October 11, 1986

Eyeball-to-eyeball, a small spot, and
        its temporary moment-to-moment hoarding stasis
Exactly!
Blue
One can cuddle with such
        after-the-fact accuracy
Night when calm gusts
Where else would one find
        the time to read as
        if in curve with reverberation
        and endeavoring
I don't know how slowly
        I first or last used
But I'm encumbered by halves
        and beatitude
Against the flying mote to
        catch its modesty or symmetry
Each mealy thing has its
        current face
A person
One can view it off
        a bird, or, so it
        seems, a currency which is
        what accuracy remains
A person constitutionally established as
        a deposit of pure reason
        leans with rhythm
Dream
Its theory is good observation
        but poor prediction

                    October 11 & 17, 1986

O observation!
What I see
And it's the little lyric
    of recessed sociability
The subconscious is close
There is an impersonal history
     of it
Any hour is my anxiety
    in space
The aesthetic room
Outdoors the clouds pour shape
    and stability into myopic interstices
These
Those—between seeing and believing
Individualism inspires an individual which
    disbelieves
The chamber on the rug
    which disbelief believes
The viscera
I can see it with
    shift and vicissitudes
The walls were thought at
    fault, interior
Loss of labor, isolation, love
But one finds it just
    as one's curious concept of
    experience exhibits oneself

October 18, 1986

12

A person drives, it is
        covered by ear
No wonder noise seems consistent
        even when it's music
It has a continuous destination
While it is impossible to
        look *at* the blue of
        the empty sky
At the same time
Normal
And at the same time
        as that
Writing, new shivers roll through
        the mental atmosphere
Flopping
The hot flotsam of scarlet
        nature conceding the falling backward
        over an apple tree
The eye is like a
        shed of staves
A certainty
Posts of ambient cones of
        attention which soak to note
        decay
The sunlight seems to be
        flapping and dry, despite the
        water
No wonder there are no
        single notes, no unique gender

But similar thoughts
In damp air which seems
        to carry sounds which identify
        with nature when it's culture

October 19 & 23, 1986

With extraordinary populist ferocity (with
        nature as hypotenuse) I've told
        a dream
Both doors are flimsy
Two women from the hotel
        staff are trying to devise
        a way of jamming the
        door by leaning a pyrex
        baking pan against the door
I suggest a different baking
        pan—it is obvious that
        none of this will work
The penitent front of leaves
        spin in description
It's proper
Silver
Poplar
Tiny golden nails come in
        the package with picture hooks
But the situation is centripetal
        in these modern cities so
        I'm worried that the police
        will figure out that I
        helped the prisoners escape in
        time over the accidental foot
        of the tree
Even if I got it
        right I couldn't keep it
        right

I'm carrying a white curtain
      (a door substitute) on a
      rod—I who can't keep
      a joke
Everyone knows I'm in love
The din is incredible (because
      of my present concern for
      feminist issues) "like leaves"

October 23, 1986

The tree is a convicted
        musician with precision
An exit
Zukofsky says, "Emphasize detail 130
        times over or there will
        be no poetic ... "
Creak, droop, racket
An uneven evening passes suddenly
        (there is a difference) between
        the convincing movie and the
        rapid, recurrent movements conducted on
        the street
It would disturb you if
        you could possess them
The wind sweats
Crickets
They govern by ear the
        nation of sound
Physically frequent, retreating, unarranged, lush,
        and unnerving—in flossy corymbose
        arousal growing gradually decisive
It is so difficult to
        grasp this because of a
        public stance and stress
A tree is not distributed
Not as actress, not as
        theory

October 26 & 28, 1986

17

Yesterday I saw that the
      sun was underlined
That's so blatantly perceptible a
      quiddity it reaches the pipe
But is the fear of
      tunnels also a fear of
      conduits
The maintenance of integrity ... which
      is sentimental
The horizon after the work
      day
I can't say comprehensively that
      it's dark
There's been some communication—not
      a storm—a person pitying
      itself having identified with a
      storm
With eyeing the median lines
      with the telephone lines
With moralities—one mental space
      capable of holding two contents
Some people are shopping at
      the supermarket when just getting
      acquainted
But change is inseparable from
      the account of it
The grave and maximum increments
      of denseness, patience, and rapidity
The entropic virtues (like difference,
      longevity, and velocity)
Great girth and defense

October 28, 1986

The stairs are in a
        certain relationship
The stairs are inserted
Between these rooms are
        an odor and an investment
Food
I may have swallowed the
        whole spoon
There's no whole scale
Down slope, under screen, from
        sooty magnetism, in social scenery
        saving all kinds of money,
        as the roofer says we
        will outdoors
But which one
Which heavy weather is a
        social concern on the tender
        browse of cows, on doddered
        shrubs the cover condensed over
        the person, the poem
Perfect roof
I ascend my inclination without
        introspection
Pay good for good
The whole mood
Justice (were natural objects evenly
        spread) and catharsis
There is absolutely no catharsis

October 29, 1986

Solid harbor, thick liquid town,
    where women bump around skillfully
    and with ardor
With boundaries—they are said
    to have a problem with
    boundaries
Without bodies
The progress of domestic time
    can be made—with docks
    coming right up into it
It has a certain necessity
    for winds, cups, or zinnias
Sustaining orientation
For haste
The many retentive sequences, sentences
But the person with bodily
    exercises identifies with its city
So a person is compensating,
    letting others in front
It seems to have made
    now a model of incommensurability
In it a person isn't
    satisfied when queried except walking
    expressly
A model of momentum
It is a small amount
    of time in a place
    known as an extent of
    experience

Unknown
Its sincerity is unofficial
Not an absolute but a
        continuum
It darkens and unregenerate darkens

October 29, 1986

I carry my thoughts in
      an ocular bucket
Space accumulates in a far
      larger tub
It is late at night
      and sultry in the heavy
      oval
Scrutiny without sticking rim
The little smile is on
      film droplets
Their beauty is their revenge
A worldwide solid
Solitude

    Solitude

that shows the mote, the
         rain
     and no chronology
     to train on

Of course I am exaggerating
     my unconsciousness
Between us I know as
     well
A wind hurries, a myopia
That very distant solipsism lost
     in sunlight

Back to the beginning, back
        to the background
The while

November 3, 1986

Dreams are perfect—it's illogical
        to think there could be
        mistakes anywhere in them
Nothing intended
Not unless you could say
        the psyche itself is a
        mistake
But it's natural that dreams
        don't change enough—so a
        person repeats them to other
        people
I pose a question and
        immediately the psyche pops up
Not something one would naturally
        name Patricia or Josh
Some nights I experience embarrassing
        assimilations
Wide and near, bare and
        far
There's entertainment in dreams without
        erudition in reality
Strongly competitive urges
Any immutable information is boring
A voice under the dream
        and reality develops
An invisible reality

November 4, 1986

24

Love substantiates comedy
You may be hearing the
  social increase its regularity, with
  milk, thunder, and aluminum siding
  and other evocative recurrent forms
  unconsciously conscious of the urge
  to make cohere
But being so easily influenced
  is coherent
The habit of fibbing to
  the left side, or of
  puffing in sleep
I think of a singer
  with a strong roar of
  straw so relentless and inverting
It's only the smallest thing
A person has a favorite
  food
Such is life
The urge to make copies
  is sociable, a very inviting
  use of friendly symmetry
The urge to make poetry
  which is ominous is intimate
Its sex is like a
  human hilarity for building
So it must show itself

November 5, 1986

Government is dizzy without capitals
        to name
More and more, connection takes
        space and correction
Every place the imagination occurs
        replace it with the working
        term "language"
With the distribution of blankets
It doesn't drone with anarchy,
        with getting away from people
The individual feeling voluntary all
        at once or else gradually
        —too proud of its imagination
        to view the highway accident
Witness to the independence of
        its happening an hour ago
        having that integrity
To change the city they
        must dictate predictions
There was a night I
        slept like a badger
Then last night like a
        ledger
Entire nerves—many of them
        accounted for
What do you suspect
The imagination is congested by
        irritations of the sex

November 7, 1986

26

A situation—which is a
        tableau of trivia—no detail
        too small and so lacking
        narrative
The quotidian with its knowledge
        resembled
Yes: distance
A moon on the hip
        of distance
My insistence on space, on
        sparing someone—
It's as if I perpetuated
        a fear
Just as a child has
        a fear of bears, though
        it is very optimistic
Time shut with the shock
        of departing
The socks removed from the
        bureau drawer
From the war
The man at the purple
        minute of lunch—his return
        observed from a station wagon
The removal of blankets
I hate a person's sentimental
        use of the word "play"
        as a substitute for subjectivity
The account of the river
        bank, the cave-in, the conduit

But the conduit was vertical
    and the child remained
A Broadway musical on Geary
    Street
The grandmother itself a survival
And now to be languid
    with tension, with rain, with
    revision—temporal with its hilarity
    —if comedy is memory—it
    is inadvertently empirical

November 8 & 9, 1986

When I say "equals" I
        mean brief representations of thoughts
        of like sticks—the breasts
        being prods of perception
We could add to the
        lines that form and see
        a raging daisy to clear
        our clocks, our props—equals
        being ephemera
Automobile equals portrait and cup
Portrait equals cows in a
        barn
A pond holds water with
        convex emotional functions
I can't take my eyes
        off a highway
It is a representation of
        repetition in distance afloat and
        halted at the horizon line
        afloat and halted
The barn is squandered
On the wall is a
        portrait of life in the
        mountains showing cows harnessed to
        redwoods
The emotions equal redwood trees
        in that one can drive
        a car through the older
        of them

Nearby is the chair of
      the ghost of the boy
        who lost his head
A silent head to see
      but not to remember
My memory equals a narrative
      replacement
Breasts in place
A person in its places

November 13, 1986

I meet myself rarely to
        experience the coincidence of my
        objectivity with my subjectivity
This incongruence is independent of
        the possibility that a person
        had an articulate organ which
        he called a lung
The blunt November summer—I
        could have only said so
Red and yellow language coming
        with the tongue
A big one
The year is thick and
        long and thrust
The label sticks up from
        the collar but the hair
        hides it
The place warm
The space bar worn
There's no such thing as
        yesterday which rolls under and
        holds its information up and
        forward for long
The information is like a
        balmy palpitation
I like everything at a
        level below its name

November 13, 1986

31

Can you draw a dog
        so utterly
I want to say something
        about hypocrisy
A dog and her thumb
        gauge
I mean, "to write"

Something is exactly like a
        dog tonight
The thumb scuffling with the
        light
It is between
Shadows number the wall

It is peopled and open-mouthed
I think that is why
        I learned to talk
If there is a nice
        science it is my principle
There's nothing about it that
        I can't describe

November 15, 1986

In the dark sky there
        are constellations, all of them
        erotic and they break open
        the streets
The streets exceed the house
On occasion the body exceeds
        the self
Everyday someone replaces someone and
        someone's mother is sad so
        as to exceed
The bed is a popular
        enclosure from which to depart
Outside the stars are stunning
        —touching
It is a question of
        scale
It is erotic when parts
        exceed their scale

November 15, 1986

The vertebrae crackle down the
        pentatonic scale
Attacked by white, dessicated and
        exact
Something is happening, the eyes
        don't speak to the brain
A drop of water is
        thrown off by the stove
The grass pocked with repetition
        is clothed in sweat
There's a slit in the
        soft coast and insomniac sand
        washes through it
A sign sweats over the
        doorway (thus gradually all things
        eventually maintain each other)
Biological destruction inevitably leads to
        fetishism
But to be honest I
        do understand a few things
        about music
Historically the thing about neighborhoods
        is that they tend to
        be abandoned
Their "thingness" depends on their
        surroundings—on not being there
Actually, the blue of the
        sky seems to lack "thingness"
        but not crackle

Now the woman is singing
        just like a large motorcycle
In fact it is intact
        when it rains

                        November 17, 1986

In the light of the
        sky (as marked blank the
        dream) I anticipate the poise
        you anticipate—love
Its time slang skin torrent
        pink soot fallacy bosom
It lifts its bazoom, in
        uprisings
Things are loved several times
        in actuality
And in reply
From below the two brows
        of the breasts an eye
        looks
Slim spaces (no greater arbitrary
        praises) and a small loan
        keep like minds and make
        them friendly and indigenous where
        they sleep
They are washing their weight
        for sleep

November 20, 1986

36

Some mortals go by on
          the street
Light knocks the great night
          inland to its waist from
          Eighth Street to Tenth Street
          independently
Home is jargon for bird
          in your lap
People see faces in everything
Through the window overlooking the
          red-rimmed yard
The form in an apprehensive
          description
The bare limbs in winter
          of somebody branching spread before
          the reflected white light
One gets sleepy without identity
          —with frustration
But I feel the anti-anti-sexuality
          of looking at the leaves
Not me, in light

November 21, 1986

What is the use of
      yesterday
When I call it sweetie
      it behaves sweetly
And the witnesses plink

My portrait is a bowl
      and I tap it with
      a spoon
The pitch varies with content
It drones predictions as needed

And here all my worries
      are history
But generally this requires money
      (that kind of memory)
The container of the century
      makes a low note

The face head-on conveying expression
      has no nose
I admit that my past
      takes persuasion to be the
      case
Percussion—it must have ears

I will call them beauty
        —the breasts are eyes
Last night I saw the
        bulging smile
What thinks to move its
        use

November 21 & 22, 1986

The world showed and it
     received worldwide attention
There are its spouse and
     memorabilia
It is a movement and
     finds itself following itself swarming
     over the window frame
Where will it all preclude
The crowded hospital, smell of
     chlorine, a loud man prototypical
     of a lewd man in
     dream
I ask my spouse never
     to die and he promises not
     to
But let us economize
Muffled, facial, scooplike details move
     the community behind the curves
     under the rain
Now it is 25 seconds
     before the rain begins
Funny to say so
Coming from a long line
     of young women
The changing of light in
     a wall of weather
The impatient who is well
I wondered, did you ever
     wear bandages to school
The very normal poet laborious
     on a convexity

The romanticization of limping, of
      sea-shells, of tenderness as
      erotic curiosity, of battered paper,
      of the paternal typewriter
Motherhood is so much information

November 24, 1986

I get mortally warmed up
      when I write the cold
      of poetry against the rocks
      on the ground
There is rain in the
      pock and wavers across it
Personality is a worn egress
To somewhere in particular, a
      soil point
One unit of rain taken
      by dictation
It raises this question: do
      you
Do you sometimes want to
      be disembodied
A dream of one eye
      to another
Repetition is a form of
      friction
A prediction—as of extreme
      cold in oncoming excitement
The person for its chance
      of enhancement

November 27, 1986

A scene of some things
        logically united—robins
Survivors—indicative of having pleasure
Dotted, discontinuity, slab, cognitions—these
        aren't pretty words
(I imagine myself watching)
Self-righteous, authoritarian, and mercenary
(I *am* watching)
Spread and independent—the person feeling
        compromised, as if it were
        a movie
Chamber and barrel
Rocks are indefinite
I feel queasy
I don't wake easily from
        movies
There is some object of
        delay—a discovery which moved
        me to tears

November 29, 1986

43

At x o'clock I shook
       the radio
It is a fixed point
       and a great sentinel
The assistance that society was
       made for
And alpha prospects require alpha
       patrol
The noisy whispers of an
       open faucet, a boiling egg,
       and an electric clock come
       from the next room
The sound of withdrawal when
       the front door is being
       unlocked
The way gulls pump themselves
       up in the air they
       look like they're waving a
       thick magazine left in the
       sun
An idea left in a
       crate
I've thought that many times
       —myopia is psychosomatic
The universe pours through a
       funnel whose spout wobbles
The universe is endless but
       it splashes out unexpectedly
And my fate is convex
       like an eyeball

November 29, 1986

Indecision
But I can hold it
        in the test of time
My being undecided, indecisive
Improvisation slaps till the fresh
        rose comes to face again
The world is cold and
        bears wild description
I keep a half-day behind
There it's exposed
But there's no keeping a
        horizontal back—it's spontaneous
Scrupulous in vain
Lax rich wind
Larger golden bosoms tumble in
        it
Also, the wind is round
It surrounds the sides of
        things to recognize by pocks
        and sounds
By moisture, by posture
The faces where it'll always
        be of things again

December 2 & 3, 1986

I closed my mind
I lie close to the
      wall near a window in
      order to sleep with objectivity
      and modesty—those pleasures which
      are contradictory
A dream is an apprehensive
      reminiscence but I think it
A scene
A lascivious sight
A larynx
A space in throat light
Persons exhibiting, and their eyes
      giving pleasure to indecision
Never the same holds true
      descending
Separation is mere escape
In a dream there is
      calculation or a situation
But sleep is an inexcessive
      oblivion
The horizon line is a
      spring
The world is short
The clouds are skin
A person has deliberately to
      keep all that can be
      seen in

December 5, 1986

I see clouds to do,
        caves with wanting to be
        a meteorologist
Cows to do
Whenever I'm forced I'm bored
But this posture inclines one
        to feel elated
A person riding through enumerations
        and sprockets
There is a calm to
        do, a number of contradictions
Are words more often divided
        by music than music by
        words?
A background might be a
        blue, and culture its copy,
        its vertical
Of no books, of things
        which might be inconceivable
The eye of the passenger
        in the moving car can't
        rest on anything, it is
        shorter than reality

December 6 & 9, 1986

47

It is obstructive to be
        round against the lightness of
        the wall
A social encounter not seeming
        to happen as it will
Nations blossom and reward from
        the vines of latitude and
        the individual person swallows the
        pace
Where else would I find
        the space to read
Deliberately to keep the sensory
        and the world apart

The open sky is blue
        with storage, its waves receding
        violently through the trees
And for whom never to
        tell
Two people cannot be bare
        at the same time because
        they have to exchange visibility

December 9 & 10, 1986

I'm being inappropriate again
I was, having been wisecracking
        warmly, sincerely, candidly, for how
        long
Let us not be hasty
The mouth opens on an
        agate
The beach is named of
        it
A person could make a
        movie of it, everyone with
        its twin in sufferance
There is that in poetry
The approach of a great
        improvement
The sound of the set
        of footsteps like ice cubes
        dropped in hot water

Shelter and respite are not
        what's intended by exaggerating the
        reality of oneself
Elated or near-twin but unvindicated
Vengeance is meant to nullify
        or separate like cattle from
        hydrangeas or rain from its
        supplicants or a conquering leap
        from this century
The bathos of desire for
        it

Lighting by trees
Flattening by depictions of an
        industrialist in a cauldron
A fiction of factors on
        a film
The animals (not dogs) stampeding
        backwards to laughter
It's not in their eyes
Writing by putting a leg
        over a knee is animal
And again it is also
        mineral
It is anatomical to repeat
        but the time isn't right
The times aren't the same
So poetry isn't a reminder

December 10, 1986

The psyche circulates
It takes contemporary floating genuineness
        to capture and assume
A woman at window seen
        sees psyche-like—trees on glassy
        luster and transparent self
Movement appears to fill the
        constant landscape, too
With irony and recourse, head
        and case
I can say that I
        do not intend to be
        the end result of anything
Still the city is enticing
        and angles for the psyche
So which is the more
        personal, expectation or repose
The psyche uncertain and humane
Mineral is a mental category
It is a moral category
        in a certain metaphor
When we suggest we'll speak
        of sex, sex is everywhere
The psyche is lagging and
        inaccurate in its head
We cannot help but run
        sex gently over the word
        head
The open mind
The bending of the head
        to see better

Spectacles to improve the eye
The eye to improve the
  psyche
A person perceptible in its
  silica reflecting on the street
  at night
On the excerpt of an
  attention, a dark outline

December 10 & 12, 1986

Unorganized octave ashes scattered in
        the humid light
The unblinking ears are their
        damp confidant
The poem is not natural,
        unnaturally desired and saturated
The relentless obligation of seductive,
        descriptive, and corrupting perceptions
Of some eternal, never-ending, everyday
        task

December 13 & 14, 1986
January 6, 1987

The fern rooted in ash
        in the fork of the
        tree
In an inch
A symmetry from penises
The sharp eye of work
Or its confidante

A person has its past
        to declare—relentless saturation
Or its passage—there is
        volition
The confidante is interposed—it's
        all a connection
Mother-equivalence is naturally desired
        in small contrasts
In situation
In practice

January 6, 1987

Do you patrol? outside the
        self? around a body and
        the follicle in which it
        stands?
Or cell?
Request?
Have you reverted?
All memory of having looked
        is loose
It is so cold parallels
        wobble in the chamber whose
        grain drifts
A sign on the fire
        door says silence
A sign on the floor
        says come in
Patrol (but there are no
        opposites) is narrowing
But I was not moving
        anywhere on my feet
Within such fear of death
        if it is a thrill
        to cease
But in the succeeding request
        I ask decease to be
        stable, not diffused or decreased
The cell of description of
        anything (and virtually uninterrupted)
Her death in a beginning
It is in a prolonged,
        ruthless, unguarded kinesis

The cell in shifts
Cells in drifts
So we're feeling a loss
      but not a conclusion
The smallest unit of imagination
      in time, a retrospection
A unit of space so
      small it seems to be
      going backwards

January 14, 1987

If reality is simply that
       which is accessible to reason
       when it folds over and
       it sticks up
Then sexuality is very optimistic—
       a very optimistic interest
It is a cyclops with
       a sharp eye for the
       apparent position and the actual
       position
And a working eye
Until we have a whole
       landscape of undivided situations
Although beauty is divided somewhat
       freely
The boundaries between me and
       the rosey cobblestones and leaves
       are nowhere parallel
But slide who are insatiable,
       genuine, solemn, looming
The ghost is only the
       poor attempt of nature to
       present herself as me in
       the language of inquiry
The naked breasts we call
       night and day or me
       and not-me
Inseparable from exposure, inspiration is
       what the ghost contained or
       could supply

Qualified praises—flesh rises to
     an emotion
The reasonable outlook, knowledge
It is based on acknowledgment
     in the end
Provocations
Justice, joy—if a cyclops
     pertains squinting and springing coincidentally
     upright until partially blinded
Of anything that is, there
     might be more

January 16, 1987

Are you elated?
Consciousness is an impertinent fighter
I myself don't regret practicality
It's bundled in the gulf
        between consciousness and fact
Acre, bounds, and empathy
Fact is an impertinent fighter
        too
Introspection is at a standstill
        —incompatibility makes me pensive—stationary
Pouncing on substance and crush
        I think
I am in a sit
The words are unseated self-reflective
        sensations of it
The elated delta, where its
        silt is always moving
I find myself in a
        good mood for chores, the
        beginning of previousness
Where that is commendably occurring
Myopia isn't laborious
Elated at a space in
        an end-to-end situation

January 18, 1987

Write worldwide—with the muscular
         power of uncertainty—and approve
         the world
Everything is subject to visibility
         and the represented model is
         wobbling
Living things in their redaction
         decide to yodel
Thanks to a psychoacoustical transformation
         they laugh
Ah! dark clipping shifts
Never alone in the chest
         tone
The unit of anything which
         will increase
An elation from weather is
         anti-anti-feminist
We make the advance which
         is sexual
One woman friend feeling embarrassed
         at the nudists' beach
From embarrassment, hidden in an
         embrace—we invite it in
The least unit of shape,
         oath, hover, farmhouse, many people's
         walking with traffic passing, green
In the park, wanting to
         see every painting and not
         to miss the gorillas

Such is the romance of
        the lack of improvement
It is obdurate but not
        leisure

January 19, 1987

This is very authoritative rain
Justice is flowing
The logical is promised impulse
    —but so communicative!
These words must be consistent
        with nature
One can't organize suction
The asymmetrically engulfed clouds harden
        in the rain
Logic rises in the hollow
        political side sunk in the
        flowing sky
The future has no bottom
        —or this appears to be
        Freud's opinion
And such romantic motherhood—some
        children sorting buttons and others
        cutting pictures from magazines
The puddles all cracked like
        eggs
Judgment precedes intention
A daughter named Canada
A son named Radical
There is a chaos to
        the soaking of the clouds
        if we only knew it
A culture that is not
        —actual as though it were
        actual
The future is natural—a
        history of ideas   *January 21, 1987*

The rain is falling over,
       each rain separately so there
       are tangles and therefore puddles
January—given in—is a
       relief
The woman gets home before
       dark at last
It is far wider than
       an egg
Function bends (the heart is
       a shell then)
But there's no time to
       divulge
The shock of difference in
       rain repeatedly
Discontinuity lets her undo
Over the rain of strings
       a thought
I thought I had said
       too much about discontinuity and
       the sex act
Failing to introspect
Failing to make a fetish
       of a specific thing
A big if
No neutrality
So people become different about
       what they eat—and then
       go on to flirt by
       cooking it

A pronounced soup
And a description—please give
      me a description

January 23 & 27, 1987

Avarice culminated in explanation ... the
        plug
It's hospitable ... so, material
In my feeling propaganda, I
        was ...
It's optimistic to xerox ... pounce ...
        ornithologize ... where poetry does not
        resist alone in books ...
Or coin: a circle and
        lid ... means the trajectory
The trajectory is eager for
        more reality and more recognition
Strutting with explanation ... with characteristic
        restlessness
I could not remain long
        from home ... for sight and
        cell

                    January 27 & 28, 1987

Many parts of experience displace
        each other in a person's
        life—and still it manages
        to light the pilot light
A person's father thus feeling
        pleased with himself at the
        restaurant suggests a person eat
        steak
That's another life
It happens when I housekeep
Terror of drain—but curiosity
        too—necessitating a telescope and
        dark
The back aches at its
        contrite hump
Scaling the fish, bent
Women of my mother's generation
        having their hair done, submitting
        as to medication
The poem is the becoming
        exhibiton of its own language
It comes only in part
        in parts
Because of what women like
In metonym

January 28, 1987

A cell cannot boast stable
        achievements
If one can say (if
        one can) that the wind
        has a stitch, the leaf
        is without one
Sleep without opposite
A call
A person inquires—
"Who visits the babies?"
The bulb of thought and character
        is shining—flickers
Our inquiries continue—as in
        a honeycomb
Confines
The provocation is a buzzing
And the person is behaving
        in a drifting skin—the
        future
It isn't a verification

January 30, 1987

Jitters occur in the transfer
        of learning
No less of this will
        I say
This is the way I
        want to go in and
        out of heaven—with depth
        perception
Windows full at five p.m.,
        my skull a place
Except that I think of
        space as the more exciting
        skill coming back with greater
        cells
And such is my complicity
        that I go without a
        clock
For the sake of my
        eyes I fake deafness
Then how much time is
        excess

February 4, 1987

There is a chance to
        blurt out to enjoy the
        view in an express expression
Justified nights and trembling
        lips
The sea with anger, a
        swirling cabbage
A world of bohemians, hemoglobins,
        behemoths
Humans learn by imitation (or
        sometimes counter-imitation, as with those
        who suffer sea-sickness) and vengeance
With a little more description
        I could gain
But then, going long distances
        in the car, I am
        over-taken by *le grand hypnotisme*
A lift of the head
        insufficiently deictic (though it's a
        case of *deja vu*)
The rainwater thrown clear
The route permitting one to
        forget with total recall
A person opened a door
        on the right side—her
        unforgettable embarrassment
All the female ones were
        officious on that side
Automatic, so stationary—liking to
        throw out empty boxes

Droplets on the window throwing
      faces
Nothing then—with its loud
      apples—penetrates the horizon

February 4 & 7, 1987

An orientated person writing appears
        to face north, so going
        from the west (but creating
        an accumulation)
A midday glare, an avant-garde
Very abstract
The security guard and its
        cups of butter—with inviting
        capability
The earlier guys who made
        certain that one could use
        words like fuck and shit
        but did something that resulted
        in this
There's no dogma out of
        this predicament
It might have turned up
        out of anywhere
All the nameable causes of
        my material
Even *glasnost*
The poem can make me
        a public discussion of my
        causes

February 7 & 10, 1987

71

A patch of psychology between
        flowers of the economy
There is politics to everything
        that hangs
Plants, entailing rain—like kisses
        and more economy
Sentiment sticks in the form
        of anything—don't laugh, whose
        fault is that
A writer singles out of
        any situation its grass
Unarrested, uncombined
The witness to the materializing
        cup
What's blue is introspective—singer
        knowing how feet feel, baby
        knowing where money's gone
Eating peaches from a hole
        in the pocket
Dry money hung up after
        burial
Blade
The word is new for
        each successive task

February 10 & 11, 1987

Waters water with consistent reference
        and pulp unnumbered clouds
Streets' pieces turn—I think
        for eighty-four years
The readers' attentions divide down
        the sides of the bodies
        between
Is blue yellow plus something
A person who had never
        seen a plant would not
        understand
The snug continent is an
        organ, a peach
The thuds of the peaches
        teach number, the number of
        a structure whose twigs are
        many sounds of life
It didn't rain by convention
The window stands aimlessly behind
        me
The rain smells like steam
        rising from cooking rice
Water, pulp, perceptual life span,
        reader, body, vegetable, continent, genital,
        apricot, number, twig, rice, window,
        steam, rain—all neighbors
With and down plus who
        many are always by moving
        with aim

February 15, 1987

73

There is a slow and
       heavy yellow substitute for the
       dead of night
I couldn't figure out how
       to mechanize it so it
       ground
The sun flounces in its
       own light
Forward! like a criminal before
       an execution to two half-naked
       persons
Comparison sets them apart
"I wish you all the
       best, my friends, but the
       best is unavailable"
Monotony, autonomy, melody, coincidence—(I
       want to indicate both blind
       chance and clear density, but
       really this is about introspection)
       —with many prominences and rolling
       in exchange
I can combine a long
       time span with a short
       one and assume the form
       of a pair of eyes
That hour, and just us!
       —the system has triumphed

February 17, 1987

Unlike it
Should itself?
It recently describes its trying
        to be precise
An apple singing in its
        bucket—to be precise, no
        apple singing, and the bucket
        red-rimmed
The metal of what applies
Is it more or less
        discontinuous to describe
Nature is worldwide—no, but
        everywhere there are convexities
Deep and sound cavities form
        under every mineral
Eyes, breasts, hillocks, turtles, cars
And sound itself—a universal
        vocabulary of operative hums made
        by plants
Objectivity modified by the desire
        not to communicate—but it's
        impossible not to communicate
And so on, personed by
        words
Then out comes a perfect
        tongue
The long one in the
        rain
It is a hardly possible
        pad

                    February 17, 1987

75

This is my fortress consciousness,
        that is anxiety which has
        repeatedly claimed credit for it
The supply wriggles
The secluded clod that's exposed
        to the sun crumbles without
        interruption

There is a proximity from
        where I am abstracted
A relief
A person refusing to sleep
        not for fear of a
        dream but for fear of
        missing or forgetting it

The time out of which
        I'll never drop is a
        skin
It's fate to be personal
        and wide awake
The objects of love get
        separated from the elements of
        love—why do they do
        this?

Do you spill liquids over
        the tip of your tongue?
        or do you pour them
        rather, back farther in the
        mouth?
On me suffusion mounts
Where do sounds entering your
        ears meet?

                    March 3, 1987

My head, it is a
        threaded egg
All those with heads of
        eggs are females

New again
Guardian buds

A slowly gathering psychology augments
        the fun of writing
It is a full head
        that breeds the most carrots,
        propaganda, birds, affection, snapdragons, autobiography,
        steam, kindling, horizontality, cotton, orifices,
        and credulity
The question "who?" disappears

In short, I promised to
        be here and here I
        am to be found
To add a head

And hear the landscape

March 3, 1987

The cold implodes and my
        ears suffuse
I think I hear a
        head and a monoped
I'm convinced that it's stepping
There is no equal to
        this bundle of identity: "I
        am Goya," a citizen
Cruelly contrasting, endowed with transitions
        and enmity, a citizen
Introspectively, a head, a wall
An overt misgiving
There is talking in Bach
A citizenship called Bach in
        walks
The one to the right
        goes against the rain
The mines
There it is, really a
        circumstance, though diffusing
And frustrating
The experience that is not
        necessarily there

March 10, 1987

The net of nerves spread
    out from a tree on
    (Name of a Modern Martyr)
    Street is all that remains
    of that prevailing person
It is vines without satisfaction
    to be dead
Such a thing as sleeping
    in their hammocks
Glinting
The proclivity of the tip
    of the head is to
    try to point to itself
A person needs closer introspection
    than that to catch itself
    doing so
Big, more diffuse, I hope,
    than blank, the eyes apply
    pressure to the mind by
    sinking
The whole skull feels like
    a squeezing eyebone
Then there's a heavy dog
    inclined through the wet window
The sight is salutary and
    came to mind inclined with
    the dog

Transit divides the vines and
        the waste of music that
        is love
The cleft contains the flow
        that issues from consummate waking

                    March 14, 1987

Clog hours measure, that broad
        duration, that morning's a unit
        of content
Clocks cross points quaver value,
        I *am* judging, the poem
        could be
A unit of cognition poised
        within and a term in
        moral philosophy

Hourly intimately shifting blades with
        total veracity as I describe
        an idea
That is, in my language
        a cup, the very grass
        and encounter
The clairvoyant might uncover—bending
        worldwide with squinting, headlong, in
        my head

What do they point to?
        through a crooked circle—the
        last hour
A volt, the tongue in
        a compass, a noise in
        the grass
More, amorous apprehension—it moves
        with periphery, it eyes measure
        and repercussion

The hours move with shore,
>   it yaws between extremes, foreshortened
>   period sensitivity
The rain's in the way
>   I stare into, the sawtooth
>   which marks
More, one small change, pushing
>   the continuity of all that's
>   in range

March 17 & 24, 1987

Love is the stranded ticking,
        that condensation
It's a peach brass that
        rings
The order of outer hours,
        or of slippage
You'll be able to give
        to someone (if there is
        one)
A portrait of a person
        idealized in its porosity
The drop of its voluptuary
        patrol
To omit mention of tickling,
        of the comical, of the
        intensely disagreeable shock when any
        sensations are interrupted, of the
        voluntary but innate tendency to
        move about, of the pleasures
        of a slow crescendo simply
        as such, and of mere
        distinctness ...
It would be a fault,
        an impatience
A fault of the eyes
        themselves

March 25, 1987

84

Hefty and conjugal—come over
        air!
Nerves keep us separate
Charged closets and dark batteries
        of sound
Time is storage, with time's
        increase
The bulk of something lost
        in storage

Disintegration is the gain of
        thought
Not distance—it is much
        later
There is more air in
        the air
Time—it has billow
Motes, chop, swell, and bubbles
        of wet light
Minutes are intermittent widths to
        keep us separate but always
        filled by their hefty and
        provocative widths

                    April 8, 1987

                        85

Anger is storage, with time's
      decrease
The person is gasping with
      explanation
Claustrophobia is its gloss
Confidential knowledge, wet rock, low
      notes, the stucco wind, the
      mind affirms everything
And I got a thrill
      from its deliberations
Many small movies being shown
      on the skin from many
      small projectors cause a tingling
      sensation and insomnia
Encloses space

The ocean is in the
      doorway
Wallpapers drip
Mood is confusion, and eloquence,
      and recurrence
A memory of rooms from
      the middle out—such is
      their containment
My thought is a prospect
      of increase, not attainment
The clock in it with
      which we never socialize
Too little danger, too much
      love   *April 12, 1987*

Cutting off the horizontals—language
        put us there
And I don't think I'm
        wrong
The one who put his
        soul down my ankle in
        research
If the whole body were
        an eye, then its soul
        would be vision
Your light on the river
        because it changes
The space bent between us
        can be used for magnification
        (distance)
To the nth power (splendor)
        we can watch
Eyes, credibility, and therefore syndromes

The impossibility of satisfying oneself
        is part of language
What is the problem with
        metaphor
Sometimes there's too much continuum
        and there are too few
        moments
The impossibility of solitude occurs
        because of that nervousness

                        June 2, 1987

87

The wives are androgynous words
Guards
They attribute lack of soul
      to the isolation of the
      several waves

Now what is love?
It obliges me to say
      a few words
Sometimes one goes blank with
      chastisement

Emitter of comparison
Is it more important to
      discover that it is or
      what it is
A just fantasy confines my
      thoughts

Form could mean force or
      stark enormous frame
The wave with the coiled
      whiteness vanishes but it's bewildering
      to look after it so
      far below
Passing through all levels of
      sanity

June 30, 1987

Bulk and seeds—they time
        at this settle of the
        year to that suggestive state
        of sleep
We all doze on the
        inclined plane of credulity
The blue changing to color
It's snug to see an
        object that's obscured
One head basking in the
        sun in July, another buried
        in trembling soil
A tremendous dirt supports the
        light

It is possessive to be
        eye-catching
Here is a sequence of
        broken changes and there another:
        biography
Metamorphosis and its objects—they
        part
A wider, obdurate drop between
        a person and a rock
        or a person's life
It always moves
The sound of a person
        passing by moves the eyes
Everything gripped by the world,
        or by a small part
        of it   *July 12, 1987*

When I get nervous I'm
      narrative
Chronological
Begin again
See life dissolving vegetate again

The perpetual green and yellow
      take shape in different and
      combined tips of light
Like a moth in an
      episode
There are no words closer
      to the intimate resemblance than
      these
Of whose method in our
      work we can create
Footfalls
Perpetual divisions in the widening
      fact for page and transportation
      in grass

A person has no place for
      revolutions of oblivion
Only time
Two persons didn't meet at
      different times
They time material, are sexual

August 3, 1987

Prove the world
The separate, profiled bulb
Broad sun, it is the
        greatest document
No head for fallibility!
I don't know of cells
        without full world
The weather having fascinating temperatures
        in their aerial decency
My universe of thought is
        involute
Half of it is time
        and the other half is
        in time too
So that my worry occurred,
        the surface contains turns
Who am I?
Having an emotion of solipsistic
        piety
Containing surface, itself containing turns,
        and so on

Grain and drone, truck and
        thorns
Gull, obituary, urine, scope, batteries,
        watercress
Collaboration
Pasture
Greet you and must be
        vacated   *August 10, 1987*

91

(*Elegy*, for K. B.)

This augmentation of infinity a
            death
But incomplete
We shouldn't stay in one
            spot to look at it
            but ...

Early one morning made perceptible
            three trees, no noise to
            hold the air ... the list
            is not complete

I want it, where something
            has affinity to it

There is life and then
            occupation of place
A gulf that drawing goes
            such
The skies are wide tines,
            blue and blue always receding

From solids, midday, no overlapping
The middle
That we too might gradually
      arrive at a life, a
      whole
Which speaks for itself and
      has no further explanation

August 10, 1987

One thing that I think
        about melody is the ordinary
        coincidence
Anything that repeats must be
        a childhood to affect you
The squall is resting on
        the poplar, quenching

Perhaps there's not enough change
        in civilization, or proportion
It gives you the feeling
        that the thing you love
        is not as important to
        you as it is to
        someone else
The coincidence (lots of sound
        sounds very much like water)
        is independent

A water involutes
It unwound the last time
Life after sleep—there too
        we have genitals and mental
        findings

The condition in an adulthood
     until it coruscates
The air is stalled in
     the emotion
The proportion

August 15, 1987

The bone of communication is
    hollow
The rain reminds us that
    we were formerly indoors with
    spines
At the top of the
    mind, abstracted from its wild
    contents—there is your rational
    movement
The mind dismantles its incarnation,
    distilled and engineered
Sex, if you have need
The eye is virtually empty
    in a strong sunlight
Retrospective brightness and interpretation booming
    in a clear mind
The wanton consciousness of consciousness
    or variable consciousness vibrates
Nine
Resonance
You spoke behind the cold
    water pipes of something infinitesimal
    or uncalculated
The changing of rain
The air filled and blown
Of residence
The state of consciousness is
    transformed into a single will,
    into several wills
A million wills

August 17, 1987

The poem is a correct
        metonym
The landscape does have microtude
That stone (pointing to a
        stone) will tell of the
        theft sooner than I

But again this is an
        imploding series, the skull in
        its soul in its skull,
        etc.
Existence is endemic to the
        desired object
I go between stones in
        order not to be trampled
And so I remain as
        private as my arm—that
        outstanding fact

Raised and it must be
        owned
The tree is pierced by
        a neck—for the most
        part taking place within the
        head
On close scrutiny it is
        at a distant place (the
        head)

August 21, 1987

I cannot separate lucidity from
        undressing
A swamp so much farther
        from the sky
Either the sky will achieve
        cessation or it is slowly
        raking

The body taken from the
        mind
Where are your shoulders and
        your hands, your color, face,
        and, while I speak, your
        ... everything?
The skin is the only
        possible means of keeping the
        different pieces together

How far down the body
        does the blushing go
The phenomenon sought is the
        very act of looking for
        it
Sky—it occurs in many
        alignments but otherwise it can't
        be seen

The thought of everything I
        want to read causes a
        kind of ache above the
        jaw
A spasm of oblivion
When you know what to
        do, it is ambition

August 22, 1987

I woke myself when the
        ghost came in
Actually I spoke to myself
        saying, "Wake up, you (I)
        are afraid of ghosts"
I once saw a ghost
        in an easy chair but
        he was a friendly one
Not demonstrating premonition
But even the words in
        the thoughts are more objectlike
        than processlike
The very light is reduced
        by evaporation, transit, syncopation, and
        spawning

Out there is a thing
        demonstrable
Not this one
I opened my eyes to
        a magnification
A giant enthusiasm is stuck,
        mortified
But one wants to know
        why emotion leads to ghosts
        in the first place

The self embarrasses the ghost
Too little action
I have a fear of
        premonition—description being apprehensive
The glimpse of the ghost
        of the life it will
        lead
To a person

August 27, 1987

Surf, protein, incentives, life after
         sleep
Imperatives
But this assumes one could
         have a full acquaintance with
         one's own contents

Meanwhile, we direct our studies
         to objects, which, after all
         are exertions
We worry that we briefly
         exist
An absurd thing, a loss,
         occurs
A dream immediately makes flattering
         mention of this

    Dream

    a seacoast or perpetually irritated
    forest as "a kind of
    wild justice" or "solace at
    our hissing bedside" to reveal
    the distant lively figure largely
    in silhouette of a nude
    woman who undulates and flows
    through a series of pornographic
    poses spreading her legs wonderfully
    as representative of walking on

a windy beach over sheets
or mirages of still water

The next day I find
        it impossible to work from
        memory
Form or content?—this was
        never the real problem
Light and color in the
        open air and their retrospective
A yellow bee or yellow jacket
        buzzing, struggling on the surface
        to escape the very cold
        water in an oval metal
        bucket being rescued
The person reaching under it
        with the palm cupped to scoop
        up the wasp keeping between
        them a water buffer
A water background
Any of the languages which
        throw the whole
And all particular choices are
        to light or color

September 1, 1987

103

Rude infinite sense
Nursed on sex
The feeling of suspense is
      a stiffness of the slow
      free life
There are optimisms the interior
      monologue cannot contain, the somnolence,
      with certainty

Talk is quantity
Animals without sleep
Time is transportation, sex an
      incentive to elapse—or wrap
      or glare
If I hadn't found it
      someone else would have—corridors
      are sad

Without compromising it
Corridors are air

September 8, 1987

A person made a virtue
     of her many asides, more
     like adoptions of than adaptations
     to reality
"I think I think," such
     that I make a noise
The noise of its source
     as the activation

Example one:

"Charlotte! Charlotte!"

Example two:

We distinguish the maudlin powers
     which bind our feelings of
     amusement
Let's anger the citizens of
     the snake house

Example 3:

"My mortal state, *knowing*, gives
     me no guarantee of what
     will happen"
So reality is a process
     not an identity

The watch of being believed
     fills the inner dialogue
The mother with the teacher
     drives the field trip to
     the cracker factory
What they do there has
     to constitute "work"

        Example 4:

"Rain!"
The person reported floating away,
     feeling pity for its torso,
     from its death scene, then
     being driven psychologically back
Diverted

           September 13, 1987

Water is to admit that
        the life in which it
        acts smacks
Accumulated itself under ants' legs
Sleep as it makes a
        sidewalk
Reality is incalculable but it
        can be done
Especially if, in daytime, dream
        is driven out
But however conscious the things
        they can only be known
        in a single pulse of
        numerousness

Waters
If reality is always inevitable
        and exterior to knowledge of
        it
They had half a minute
        left to spread their weight
        in light
The waves calving
Waves nascent, waves remaining
Then knowing it should be
        irrevocable and inner
Stimuli include 9) shock from
        a flash of lightning and
        136) collision with a hill

A person waiting to see
the sea and to sense
its ceaseless first halves

September 23, 1987

Serpents to eat us—a
        charge reiterated time half-formed awaiting
        vast apparatus when it throws
        off a form of consciousness
        which has since kept its
        sensual meaning
Of all external supports, they
        are the same

Or passing
A grammarian with legs on
        water leaving himself and herself
        naked to the waist

September 30, 1987

109

Viewing is a complicated bearing
            around things having been confronted
In the indistinguishable distance, that
            open paralysis ...
In the light all over
            waters blurs are interspersed and
            scratching
There is specific struggling in
            sight and knocking them together
Self-consciousness is an indignity, that
            close sequence
No blinding sum

Viewing in the greasy air,
            cups and ridges on its
            conveyance
Conjecture is an ode, rolling
Viewing, persistently and latently
It necessitates and changes a
            glow by rubbing and a
            sum by interjection
Simultaneity is only a measure,
            the one for which I
            can't find a match
There are briefer curves, the
            culmination of accuracy, and an
            overwhelming emotion of accuracy
It is like an emotion
            of multiple anatomies

October 6, 1987

It is soft to be
        a mechanical object
The inner salt is unlikeness
All day the person is
        remaining reminded (and so feeling
        granular until it's impatient)
The one you are booming
        at, who is removing pajamas
        and a fur hat
A few intermittent ice particles,
        the cold ones
It arrived at the shore
        somewhat after its dry shadow
Words, limb on limb—they
Demonstration shoots out of the
        water
The metonym is anti-platonic
There is nothing in back
        of the zenith
It is memory that's the
        opposition in thinking to what
        you read

October 13, 1987

The allowing lozenge is not
        akin
Despite sparks, lit by calcium,
        dimmed
After getting somewhere, it (somewhere)
        appears to recede without necessity
Introspection is not a choppy
        narcissism nor a paraphrase
A geranium in its rigidity
Inside the block a dog
        howling from its leash at
        a siren
And ice—
The mind climbs a collision
I can see that the
        mind is glad
Today—that's an apparent comparison
But it's difficult to examine
        it
It's as if it were
        nagging, buoyant, anew, waiting, or
        the result of a decision
        not to wait any longer
Flirtatiously grieving, whose ambition is
        thunder
Fulfillment and symptoms
A release between all subjects
It is the instant object
        —for hours in the cold

Hesitation is contorted and memory
     is its poor likeness, ribbed
     and regular, but unequally confessed
Whole sequences of perception like
     water sliding in the cold

October 31, 1987

Realism, women, and introspection—with
      the object to supply
The ugly
A person, never less
You can see that work
      is the mother of pleasure
It must be from the
      front
The exhibition
A language that exists before
      every act of squeezing
And it persists in vulgar
      reversals (echo and the air
      will stink)
The tinkering with which a
      cruelty is thought
One cannot introspect except with
      respect to something
A thought makes its sentence
      its boundless passion, the transformation
The opposition

November 2, 1987

114

On *what* do the eyes
        finally come to rest
Sentences that hang the face
The eyes winching their things
Quietly to *what*
The body is bent to
        speak of thoughts changing into
        new forms
Many thoughts are of no
        things

November 15, 1987

The person thinks by being
    aloud
That is the relationship of
    music to poetry
A single body whose function
    is to represent the queen
Which things are seen
An emphasis on a medium
    bares what is assumed
Arrhythmic, then immortal
All the mortalities merge in
    the definition of "rhythm"
Moving ruin, letters speed
There is a grouping below
    the eyes
In breast, in time
It is repetitive to be
    exceeding and effaced
The landscape brightly backlit (childhood)
    is the false loss
The rocks and the stalks
    are sharp
Even the waters, or the
    light splashing back
Sand comes back at the
    examiner
Sound—the trajectory of plenitude
The spiking
I think of the portrait
    when grammar comes (profile)

The examiner is discretely cavorting
        to itself
There is no sane availability
        of the harsh sound in
        its wake
The gradual efficiency in its
        dream

December 9, 1987

The isolation which can't be
            provoked
I.e., memory
In order to be able
            to enjoy love
But a memory is embarrassed
            by consciousness of love
In its parts (which are
            not anti-artistic) it is a
            contemporary languid but buzzing temporizing
Thinking in its gripping microtude
That genital
An independence anticipates the mind
            reader
The sampling and lamentation of
            the contemporary
I have a second half
            left without predictable effects
Yellow and a darker yellow
There are very few physical
            memories of summer but they
            always anticipate the sun
Between the trees the bond
            spun
The mind might be reread,
            fears first, with digressions
By day the telescope is
            an orifice through which sky
            flows
Pleasure is stubborn, in retrospect
Nowhere to end   *December 14, 1987*

No anecdote goes with this,
        nothing is spared
It is a prediction because
        there's sex in it
Sections
There is a sentence and
        therefore a sensation, an incorporation
The body, but it cannot
        hold
Blueness holds the sky and
        the sea is bound
Discontinuity without certainty of end
This is society, not science
Where are your polarities, your
        transitions
Only gerunds, during a seduction,
        it being a selection
I don't know where I'm
        finding it spared in the
        dry light
It is absent or arbitrary,
        where someone sprawls for pleasure
In any ramification there are
        genitals
The arboreal others and cultural
        ones to see how it
        turns back

December 20, 1987

119

Some see loud apples falling
        with less decision than likeness
It catches the night light
White line
And what of the listener?
That light is intellectually collapsing
There are such individual emotions
        that anyone knows oneself unprepared
        with half-hoping adjustment but unsolved
        cave
Heat fills the ocean with
        bed—but incompletely and brightly
        at the same time it's
        never entirely closed
There will be another dark
        in the noise with its
        funnel of amazement
Your political boom that someone
        should know
But between consecutive booms there
        are no consequences
A show, a culture, of
        elegies
They demonstrate similarity or its
        reverse, also similarity
Your similarity and my similarity,
        all of it

January 20, 1988

My sincere head is muffled
        in its mind
What does it have against
        metaphor
A thought that's a taking
        of time
Never

Each person has its own
        idea of sensuality
Constructedness
Maybe constructedness could take forever
The scent of trees and
        human problems
The scene which concentrates—it's
        difficult to concentrate on the
        motion itself
I would have to be
        reminded of myself
It proceeded—
I can't say the man
        in the myth became a
        eucalyptus tree transparently
I can't say the house
        for sale stands in the
        perceptual field of paranoia
It would have to repeat
        itself (but it can't repeat
        itself)

There is a repeat but
    it's made for response—the
    sincerest opportunity to see it

January 23, 1988

Mention rain and grammar follows
Proximity
Sometimes I feel the guilt
      of inquiry—it's a formal
      turbulence
My dream in which a
      downpour was surging into trees
A door to a boat
      flooding under a canopy
Some nights I dream the
      report of my dream as
      if sleeping in phase with
      reality in which I accused
      x of sexism to his
      face and subsequently dreamed of
      having sex with him
Conditions advancing for time to
      meet their own proximity
Time itself is a querulous
      privilege of form
A false or drenched derivation

January 25, 1988

Lines in meditation—or inspection
        —convinced of my head's substantiality
It retains a memory of
        an encounter with a coyote
Though it bobs in the
        middle, thinking flesh, feeling general
Feeling female in identification with
        a male animal
Sleep is a mere lull
        in the object, which rolls
        back into balance
Without trajectory?
This is the thought without
        its head
The crack in the wall
        of an animal profile open
        to the throat
Sunlight on the window sweating
        and through it chirps
Some middle flitters of change
        which no objections can stop
There was a mouth opening
        there in pure assent
Many self-consciousnesses—the territory stalled,
        construed

January 28, 1988

The shifting drizzle springs—there
        is no quantity, no singling
We must buy fish, fresh
        tea, and some paper towels
        next time
The silhouette goes from up
        to down
Voices accumulate around the alarm
        where a while ago they
        were singing, "Need need"
Those cool metonymies
Peppers
Fluidities
My cold digits alert us
        to our physical foreignness since
        it is pure loss
The body of saying "dear
        inquiry"
It is not one word
        at a time
One can have medicine, especially
        aspirin, as a quotidian
One takes orders—Einstein says
        there will always be poverty
        —internalized
Dreams
There are no words but
        in thinking
Of bottles there will often
        be green ones with green
        blades

I dreamed of a beach
　　　on Saturday under the sheen
　　　of water and it could
　　　keep going
But it was received, and
　　　I must have been expecting
　　　it
It was where I was
　　　privately sinking

January 29 & 30, 1988

Clear listener, kept awake and
        your subjectivity is the result
There's an itch just below
        the right eye as it
        looks at the bay and
        a map of it
Adolescence occurs *between* people
Head bathed in blue air,
        some coastline
The same discord
Something is missing someone and
        my typewriter knows me
It repeatedly postpones the present
        because it can't be done
I *will* tell you what
        adventures befell me yesterday late
        between trees
What narrations befell
Powerful forces obeyed the bugs
Books I don't even read
        remained where I have readied
        them
The terminus, a form
An egg
There are very few serious
        ones
Meanwhile the books arrived in
        a shipment of monkeys, or
        of mangos

Of bifurcations, and the trees
      rushed
The population of thrushes flushed,
      while whistling while scarlet while
      leaving

February 7, 1988

Laughing (it being resilient to
        do so though it might
        sound like coughing) at regularities
        (so sad) through the teeth
        gently I can insinuate
Something into something, in increments,
        perhaps viscous
I am a moralist—there's
        no substitute
So temporal persons confront temporary
        waves
Their smoking waterfront
The lights (passengers) flicker, judging
        the temperature (curtains of it
        hang)
It is a greasy sea,
        a moving one
It's coincidental to recognize where
        we are, what that sounds
        like
My information in a range,
        but it changed
I followed the sound but
        the thing was gone
For society I now have
        you

February 11, 1988

Color could not heal one
        of indecision
Blue is a sense of
        brain
The coat is empty but the
        the sleeves are full
Then is my little cat's
        meow in form
The car is the same
        color as my car
The nectarine with the most
        temperature in the landscape
The book contains portraits of
        the platitudes of people you've
        never heard of who have
        the rectangular names of ...
The sensation of an ant
        crawling on my face where
        there is none
Sense of name
This is a bureaucracy with
        equal doors
The discourse is functional in
        corridors
This is not a labyrinth,
        says the person with apple
        green cheeks and rosy neck,
        just meandering
Its name is very objective:
        a house is a form
        of housing

There are other forms, for
		example fruit meat
So why so sad
The rapist was seeking a
		vegetable kingdom
He said his name was
		no business
So sunnily monotonous
A knot of genuineness, of
		trust
In this case it will
		be gender specific
Dear Sir or Madam, I
		have held my present job
		for many years which were
		not leisurely ones and it
		is not a popular one
A lot of brown smoke
		meaning bushes
Meaning salary
Why scold the child who
		drew the bird with three
		wings
The child who shot it
Many women shopping and they
		will watch out to know
		the butcher's name

February 15, 1988

This is my sense of
            name and pleasure
So to speculate—what is
            the same as what
Lathered with existence after exercise
            a person is elite
It's pink and yellow
Science, duty, golden justice, and
            flame
Etc.
The bugs are whirligigging in
            the breezes of cooked fish,
            their sour milk, of putrid
            rinds of something, gristle, juice
Some of that rhythmic circulation,
            but without much horizon, is
            in the nature of the
            job (work)
At work, when I know
            what to say, I think
            it
Ours is a planet, but
            I've never seen it
Then alone, at home, in
            the kitchen where the food
            is concealed in aromas of
            salt water the pelicans crash
Arise
There is solitude throughout the
            history of literature
And someone in it   *February 17, 1988*

132

Her glass balloon and on
         it stood a bulldog
It is hers to be
         methodical—genuinely methodical
The baby sheltered under a
         showercap, sitting in the pond
The escapade when nothing happens
Dog and waters
The monochrome is gleaming with
         all the hues of reality
The authority of its story
Vicissitudes
Our temperature has such authority
         we never feel it
But judges are very skillful,
         ones who change the scale
         —our pressure and our temperature
The authority of the unspeakable
The authority with no equal
The appetite is a pleasant
         duty
Someone must be feeling it
There's no equivalence, and nothing
         can replace a blue
Saying so makes it meditation
This word in a flow
         is the metonym
The coconut
The ocean is a big
         blue conduit in constant motion

and she thought to feel
            it
But this procedure is exhausting
            in that it reflects
We can say "his penis
            escaped from his pants" but
            we can't say so of
            "her vagina"
It's unspeakable
Still one way of looking
            at this point is to
            consider it a constantly changing
            human life
And the sun its wife
An ant on every one
            of its hairs

March 5 & April 15, 1988

Under her shirt are two
        clocks without hands
Turning socially
Postmodernism is a child's room
        cluttered with toys, games pitting
        our desires against our fears
The sole object prolonged
Let's save our passions for
        something that exists, its sole
        object
Because everything is very expensive
        in enormous proportions
The freeways are extensive too
Many self-consciousnesses, none impeded, a
        rising dust
There's no horizon line, only
        horizon points, dots
Stirred
Which are your provocations—polarities
        —when caution itself is a
        tour de force
And planes to connect them,
        with corresponding skies, differentiated and
        deferred
A person forms around a
        psyche, two psyches
In a great sexual life
        they have no power to
        time

April 18, 1988

135

Tiredness for the male and
        female gives an impression of
        the present
It's incomplete, perpetually—is being
        written is unwritten and nearing
        completion, what
Do I mean enough to
        stop (which suggests a violent
        metamorphosis)
There's a strong smell of
        grass in the drought—it's
        physically pleasurable

An autonomous drought—now everything
        is close to the body
Selected letters, elastic hedges, rust,
        and a mouthful of lake
Everything is that which is
        close to the body
The plural is the science
        of distinctions

So between spaces there has
        to be motion—blue, for
        example, or nation

April 19, 1988

A sound and its swallow
        —or can that be name
        and its time
A sound without its thing
        is usually thought to be
        incomplete
A phrase jumps to its
        continuation—it is oblong like
        a person
And it has rather than
        sweet reason sexual difference

April 20, 1988

The person withholds violence in
          this erotic situation which violence
          would speed up
The rising dust is disturbed
          by a mineral
Deferral
Let us say so
By next week we'll need
          more coffee and probably laundry
          soap
A prediction—and somewhere there's
          sex in it
So this thing preserves its
          form which is motion
Suspense with motion chastising
Here a calming consonant is
          caught on a vowel but
          between words
When, by the way, I
          say say I mean write
The complex boundaries of the
          flower in the grass in
          a gulch
Number
It's because of the time
          problem (which compels us to
          talk talk) that we have
          recourse in nature

The trees are branching between
      minerals
If so
And impeded substitution

April 25, 1988

This is the female opinion
        in several inseparable places and
        I will keep my confession,
        my syntax
It's my position
Syntax is a measure, and
        on it are increments of
        pleasure
Wherein is what they register
And wide
Why to know about poetics
What to know about consonants
My containment
A moment of lumber in
        the building of a society
        for members
But it isn't space that's
        subdivided into units of a
        situation when one says legs
They might place one or
        take the place in an
        emotion
But the perambulation is coherent
        —though coherence doesn't go (being
        lovelike) without saying
This specific crisis in consciousness
Sex is the pleasure of
        inexactitude

April 28, 1988

This egg is an emotion
The sensing of a large
      amorous aptness
It is putting us in
      mind of the other things
      of most thoughts
Is "it" pleasure?
Endless it
And in defense of our
      sex

"But my darling," we said
      straddling the line between the
      artificial and the natural
If lust and narcissism are
      evil they must belong to
      social relations
Nothing economizes more than the
      economy itself
This is conduct
And in the example before
      us it exhibits lust and
      narcissism

Meanwhile, everyday life requires common
      sense insatiability
A disappearance from history
Thus the breasts are two
      entirely different thoughts

One is of tropical birds
          and the other of the
          Fire Department
Or one is of self-portraiture
          and the other of new
          tires
Thinking is a pleasant incorporation
It is an emotion of
          sex where it resembles the
          patience in travel

May 3, 1988

Yesterday I saw the sun
         sagging with assent—fat, yellow-green
         and pink
The live body in its
         spectrum
The guts to be sufficiently
         mental
We gawk at a brutality
And self-consciousness is the situation
         (stasis) of objection
She assigned herself 20 pages
         a day
Throbbing sticks, the installments stuck
         on them, the sunlight swelling
Any person who agrees will
         increase

So I am going, like
         a proper editor, to introduce
         the reader
Because culture does not fall
         into the arms of the
         first comer
The reader, with its eyes
         glued to the slits and
         its heart going out to
         me, surveys my efforts
The question is framed in
         something like words: "What is
         that on your mouth?"

She lowered her head and
      saw the grass, which had
      been almost under her feet,
      growing far below her—clearly
      reflected in it
I.e., introspected on subjective grounds,
      not just by being near
Subjectivity is not a misuse
      of substitution
Objectivity is not a misunderstanding
      of sex

May 5, 1988

For example saying so is
        really only a transition
She said, "I've got some
        information for you, things I
        found out, but the first
        thing is to get your
        coat off," and she helped
        him out of his coat,
        ran into the hall to
        hang it up, and ran
        back to keep her eye
        on the soup
Even a woman's beauty can't
        keep the sexual act
In such a case ... though
        the eyes love their things
There it is, opposed to
        violence, between the two worlds
These things are beloved like
        parent and offspring
The blue of Anna-Marie or
        Papa's prematurity
So to suppose a full
        signifier and then it is
        contravening borders
Each breast has only a
        single finger
Buttery blocks, bobbing in rocks
The rocks are scoops
Curiosities understood
So where should we stop

Certain curiosities are dependent on
       the male's considerable exercise of
       them
A smoke in the pot
       and a second smoke, a
       blue one

May 10, 1988

Sex is the jostling of
    a nostalgic crowd
They are singing of freedom
Freedom, freedom—are we not
    free?
"My beauty, your darling has
    ruined the place"
Sex is shameless precision
Everyday sex, sexes—they argue
    their popular songs
"My darling, your beauty is
    replacing irony"
All the more songs are
    turning utilitarian and utility is
    a luxury in itself
Space passes between the streetlight
    and the gutter
And I can't promise that
    what I remember doesn't come
    from the stereo
But time passes and now
    we have money
Trees
Displacement is not a configuration
    but a necessity
The quotidian passes into the
    trees

May 11, 1988

147

With a wave of yourself
        you're here with me
It's delightful, restricted, but inevitable
        yet in its unavoidably abridged
        impression harsh—if harshness and
        inexpressibility can be joined
They can't
Just at the window love
        recovers
Twilight falls
On each breast is a
        vestige of this *joie de*
        vivre
How long?
We feel our curiosity about
        the contents of a time
        zone
If you feel love for
        someone you have to show
        it, even if he or
        she disapproves
It is that guard house,
        that overtness, that blockade, that
        unit of endurance, those disproportions,
        that perpetuation, that nonseparation of
        weathers, the additional weights, and
        the waiting, unexpectedly desired

                        May 13, 1988

The child tears the bug
        apart with an awful curiosity
An outer sour eros
An inner ticking and its
        drawl
Sentience is a better solitude
The cat sensed whole has
        its trouble fitting in the
        lap with its legs crossed
The silence has its rain
        pulled back
I feel that it's disappointing
        when it's not understood
And then I have a
        migraine and a bug to
        revive, which is ridiculous
Lips, without us
Enormous—without limit
I still have the vivid
        memory of a picture of
        metamorphosis
If there were continuity some
        of it could absorb this

May 16, 1988

149

The wonderful muffledness of the
        moment of solitude which covers
        the breasts
They are both locks and
        lapses
Words—
But the moment is very
        warm—summer arrives without thinking
        although thought is intruding
Some irateness at a model
        of morality as gladness in
        an uninhabited place
Only a tombstone, a reinforcement
An unrecorded heat
Let us save our hatred
        —don't we hate?
A thought reformulates, not an
        altogether new one
It had fallen apart and
        then it followed
Almost in summer—almost—in
        summer almost
Echo and the air will
        shrink
Is this it?
Each memory isn't a thought
        that reiterates
My memories are comparisons, even
        the short ones

May 21, 1988

If yesterday was an old
      woman cooking, today is a
      seated gray sheepdog
The contained
The female of that generation,
      her salt
The streets, where they enter
      a proper noun
Like the desk and the
      deck of a ship
The ice
The idea
"Talk of mysteries!
I'm astounded by my body"
A strange matter in which
      I'm bound
An elk, a pane of
      glass, an egg
"Think of our life in
      nature—daily to be encountering
      matter, to come into contact
      with it—rocks, trees, wind
      on our cheeks! the *solid*
      earth! the *actual* world! the
      common sense!
Who are we? *where* are
      we?"

May 22, 1988

And your cheeks!
Talk of mysteries!
Think of our life in
        a nation—daily seeing mothers
As soon as they stop
        doing something which proves the
        existence of a human mind
        (such as writing in a
        notebook outdoors) the wind comes
        up
Altogether what order of magnitude?
I can look at a
        body and perhaps not be
        interpreted as the body's
"It is time…"
It is still in its
        lifetime but there is practically
        nothing to foretell
Between a reason and an
        action
The plotted and sentimental body
        in which we sit on
        a slope to admire
Discontinuity (reference) is the survival
        of our expectation
A mountain is defined as
        a rise with two climates,
        a hill as one with
        one
Everywhere color covers us with
        uncertainty

The side of a smile
        covered by the cheek
The pleasure however unchecked

June 1, 1988

Love is an unfinished "form"
        of history
Overstated, a suckled number, a
        tug
I live on Russell Street
It is a line, a
        curve
Without convergence—what is memory's
        relationship to it
We seem to remember it
        on the lefthand page—the
        one with the word "love"
        on it
Smells of atrocity—knives stripping
        the leg muscles of the
        living helpless person
Undressed to be given reason
Given heaven
We receive a flat sun, an
        upper window, swimming animals
The naked object is given
        and the azaleas advance
The torture Dante died too
        soon to write
It exceeds with only a
        brief stay between dawn and
        division
Love "explains things only to
        us"

June 4, 1988

Women and money
You can see in the
      sea over there them
They are absolutely necessary to
      motherhood
This one is less austere
      than that one—and can
      one say so objectively comparing
      blues? coins?
That one avoids the link
      between an offspring and a
      puddle
This one is exhibited with
      largesse
Mothers are given a round
      sum and an amount of
      time
The backtrack with belief
The corridor in the back
      of the car
When time is omitted there
      is something obviously wrong and
      it includes so much
Meanwhile money isn't garish and
      some of it can be
      grain
And so it is that
      mothers because they purchase so
      much—the greatest amount of
      purchasing is done by mothers
      —do it regularly, anywhere, and

very often, until it's hardly
visible, something white behind a
green medium—spring and a
cascade of peas!

June 5, 1988

To have or have no
        particular money in mind, or
        meal, or light source during
        the day
Candy money is incalculable
To know more about money ...
The most palpable self is
        the body to which selfishness
        relates
A person decomposing the unity
        of the subjective mind by
        dint of its own introspection
The body loves its food,
        its breath, its bed, the
        sexual parts of its sexual
        mate
Praxis ... ossification
There is an unsettling possibility
        of this work in that
        sex
But money doesn't give itself
        to poetry
The artistic lack of person
The hospital ... I mean, the
        university ... actually the hospital distributes
        qualities
The university distributes quantity qua
        quantity
There is money in the
        light

It was put there to
        free the hands
So the child won't swallow
        the money to speak

                    June 6, 1988

Two body parts wobble and
        hint of a coincidence
A crow on the pole
        praising character
The coincidence is an estimate
        but also an instance of
        seduction
The would-be and the actual
        eroticism—in connotation and in
        coin
Will it be halved or
        doubled now
There is a bird always
        selecting along the axis from
        specific branches in that short
        row of trees
Description, description and repeat
The commodification of time
The temporal element operative in
        every commodification
Any copy of the poem
        is guaranteed to be identical
What are the objects in
        this poem on selection
A bird within its range,
        within its relativity
A neighborhood wobbling within rain

                    June 8, 1988

The crowd is blowing in
        a solitude of all those
        present quite excited
Of each of all preceding
        ones some have faded
Some are fading and no
        longer watch with any light
        and slightly downcast eyes
Swarms
Swarms without consciousness of composition
There is a child who
        never chanced on us as
        its mother to get a
        kiss
Its further mote, its fat
Its friend is warming a
        huge coin in her pocket
She is smoothing, foreshortening
The excited existence and yellows
        moved
The spot worn through
Everyone seems to turn in
        the conduit
There is too much content
        in oblivion
So much conscientiousness which is
        how romantic

June 10, 1988

We've lived our years at
         various rates
Some are inappropriate and therefore
         we have gender
A person is time not
         speed
A person (I will call
         it you) and the low
         warm ochre color of my
         pencil
The person more pointed than
         the pen
We are very pleased
Little feet, long head—but
         well-designed—shapely and with sequels
I took with me a
         large crate of potatoes
A bank
There are many symmetries yet
         to be distributed
We got our money in
         the middle
Veering, and then subsiding
We did experience an irresistible
         normal crumble—the sex organs
         being variously funnels
And funny—substances hyphenated amid
         our experiences
Music, croak, and resumption
Substantives are not evocations but

convections—time is drawn into
the self
It is swimming after the
smallest rates and sticks

June 11, 1988

We move roughly from sex
        to uncertainty
My meditation is a silica

Sands abob in the waters
        between inevitability
Or they are tuna with
        spiders astride

Writing in mobs
Soaking

And isn't this itself the
        endless triangulation: water, thing, and
        nearing
It seems the only backlit
        method

Then going back to the
        sex forgotten, the one directly
        ahead
Smaller than gravel, more coarse
        than silt

The future is dying
But tomorrow is that to
        which the future is unequal

June 13, 1988

163

The thought can't soak apart
      from a head
Atonement's music
The matching dead
When Hegel went to Paris
      for the first time before
      his death he wrote, "faces
      ... but flickering from a larger
      crowd"
Its march and spread
The open thought
Why Hegel's head?
Hegel was a name for
      the author around it
And deeds
Choice
It apologizes for the mess
It is an object of
      consciousness, otherness
A plunge and then another
      one
We witness the distance with
      pins
The particular beauty and bathos
      of such in orders, stroking
Every person sticks up in
      its sunbath

June 14, 1988

A love has its history
    which is not too far
    removed
So the love remains
The shudder of charity increases
    love in the blood
This is detrimental to pieces
The investigation entailed a lot
    of ...
Personal intermittence
Or, rather, acquiescence
Address
Cup
What can we add to
    the form to increase it
Every sense is a tent
    yet somewhat mechanically not like
    music but like time
Won't it lock its knees
    over me
Strong breaks, the "last minutes"
    —there is no static language
    for this
Imagine a person turning kilometers
Every kilometer would start at
    a tuning hub
The broad inductive velocity would
    sweep my large society

June 19, 1988

The future will be visible
        to its particular philosophy
If so it will be
        teachable to photography
New
The rain is dependent and
        stands on many things
But no
When I lowered the light
        beam the bulb touched my
        knee
Ambition is greater than the
        sum of the parts but
        less than a tangible object
Attention is very great over
        bulbs
Such poetry is reproductive
She intended pedagogy when she
        drew the head with genitals
It is possible with piano
        muscles
The driver in the car
        ahead on a sunny day
        hung his arm out, his
        cruelty
It is a variable
Productive with half a genital
A part, and a body
        particle to which we've deduced
        poetry

                    June 20, 1988

166

The rain split the soil
        into solubles
Properties, as true as anything
        else and next necessities
How could he know that
        she wasn't a witch perfectly
        representing his mother
Her convincing storage worried him
        regardless
The steepness of the hill
        was a sad one and
        it had no address
They plotted her calcium
Her narrative
Only pigeons
Deliberately
From under the hill a
        small airplane came up in
        a fountain
One person responds by fixing
        motes, another person by floating
        them
The poem which is to
        language what the person is
        to society
But in order …
Way ahead …
Weather that gives a continuous
        or intermittent signal
The landing of ligneous rain

They abandoned the sound in
     large measure to a large
     measure
A tissue

June 22, 1988

Your thoughts belong more with
        your other thoughts than with
        my other thoughts even when
        we're in the same room
What is love?
"It's Siberian!"
We keep ourselves tenacious with
        the grip of our lesson
Sex is not an abbreviation
        nor are the sexes abbreviations
We would never be imitating
        persons of a different sex
        even our age or older
And so we raise follicles
But unfinished

So I was feeling tyrannized
The inner drift fastening itself
        about us in cold fantastic
        shapes
In calves
They come to rest
They seldom do
I was feeling those worries
        which resemble politics, the ones
        on which politics are modelled
It's often just after sleeping
The sun over from the
        cold water gives us a
        thrill or an unobtainable form   *June 25, 1988*

169

I had never really felt
      that my name was my
      substantive
Something switching in terrain
A grandmother is a factor
      in the economy of the
      stream
She's in an exchange system
      of irreversible flow
A cyclops with one eye
      but a grandmother with two
      breasts
It would have been easy
      to steal the bricks but
      I paid for them
Actually, more easy
There was a long line
      but the checker had not
      produced it
Someone saying "Mom" with rewards
One wonders whether to be
      officious about the stranger's baby
      endangering itself
The child (not the stranger's)
      listens to the story as
      close to the stomach as
      it can
The event which would be
      over when it was told
It was major
Much later—the man with

       his penis showing closing the
       gap between shrugs
The modest discontinuity
A person is keeping its
       time (balance) between the waking
       world and the sleeping one
Immodestly nagging unhappily while in
       actuality happy
In actuality actuality

June 26, 1988

It rains here in winter
        on quantity and content
In summer it thinks all
        the time
Theory is a snapping term
Someone's worry can't be independent
The traveller keeps its eye
        in its hand
To the weather what it
        writes is not a proper
        weather diary
The difference between condition and
        cognition
Drought the nation over and
        over
But the poem is a
        voluptuous measure of resources
I couldn't defer my weather
        to the walls
Its objects are phenomenal
The will is a great
        trilogy

June 30, 1988

We describe a distance on
        a tongue between fixed points
A post of rain and
        a post of grain
I'll always explain myself
The objects of the will
The filaments installed
The hairs are springing heart
But the hairs are epiphenomenal
Irritations
Blue
Blue can't be secluded
And with a kind of
        optimism I can supply myself
        with thoughts
Those increments
My silica
We will have communication but
        in that many transitions
A person to be funny
        buried itself in sand
Blowing portraits, the genital popping
        up
Other transitions, the ones between

July 1, 1988

The crossing is very soft
     where the ant is on
     its stomach
Part object, part subject—these
     are the intimates of the
     description
But as implacable as a
     privilege I digress like a
     person sunning on a rock
Crawling on and on, an
     impression of the grass on
     its inflamed palms, on its
     style
Lyricism—it makes the country
     seem far away
The different stages of it
     are so short that each
     day is a measure
A geranium is posted in
     its ground
A pelargonium actually at the
     tip, which is mottled, ruffled
The Marquis de Sade not
     having been overly orderly with
     his notions, having all of
     them
Synchrony is a form of
     cruelty
The lover of nature is
     afraid
Nature cannot protect impressions   *July 3, 1988*

The object is itself but
        always ceasing to be itself
So space has its sensualists
Boom: soap: a fountain in
        a potato
But compare this with oranges
Angels
Intervals
There is a hawk to
        that field's tail
There is a wedge to
        this twilight
But no real temporal competence
Poetry lessons
Sleep is not an homogenous
        affair
Imagine that all experience can
        be divided into parts but
        with the body and the
        mind always on the same
        side
Only there is no one
        to stand by and observe
        it
Dreaming in a wakeful state
        —spotters at listening posts set
        among sunflowers
That kind of intentionality
Households use air for tendency
        and heat for rising
They keep keeping

Static
Everything—all—anything
Aftermath
The aftermath is dislodged from
     its position

July 4, 1988

We don't *understand* what we
          hear, we *anticipate* it
A hill in sunlight only
          slightly stubble
The trees can only partially
          dapple the blue shadows of
          the sunlight
There we were where x
          meets y—we moved and
          they met again
Sex is very cold to
          be inventive
Slightly thread
Placing an unfamiliar sound somewhere
          —under a binding left or
          right intrepidness
The pleasure of mentality is
          enormous
The wind a gorgeous barrier
          itself to deafness
We were seeing a bird
          in its cover—I had
          a sensation like love of
          schoolbooks
Very sore toes
In the atomlike continuum, out
          of occupied trees
The tones were moodless—interwoven
          with credibility
A sentence isn't chronological

But a person becomes envious
       from observation—some things being
       unequal so she can't simultaneously
       imitate them

July 8, 1988

A description of hazard, theory
What then doesn't wobble towards
        description
A person might ask if
        its mother is a natural
        or a cultural thing
A bundle or a burden
        of properties
There is heat in obesity
        equal to the thumping in
        a bulb which is purely
        reproductive named "Mom"
It isn't aboriginal to make
        as much noise as a
        theory of description
The bees are working backward
At first a man was
        there, but he was pregnant
        and didn't want to be
        stung by the bees
My personal mother was outlined
        when she got out of
        bed
Unfalsified
She expected a letter
An abalone
I was walking on the
        sides of my feet in
        the sand, trying not to
        make tracks identifiable as those
        of female feet

Thus I'm completely unembarrassed
There's a long way to
        go judging
The waters are bulging with
        description
Glossy with stillness, cups gliding
The waves sucking up the
        rising sand close so it
        stands but only into part
        of the wave above which
        there's an effect of red
        glints, as in green rock
Considering how the waters differ
The position prepositional, of deferral
So it's inevitable to wait,
        to be punctual
So it's a theory of
        duration

July 13, 1988

The explorer is inclined to
        look off eye-level
The pitch of description leaves
        him or her feeling suspended
Hardly here and there a
        bee to be seen
The person around its own
        spine or victim and looking
In the sleep, the eyes
        often cast up
They go to horrible heights
        for the motion of dreaming
The genitals are attracted by
        space and time—by what
        happens in them
The cloud drifts away—the
        event taking place is not
        affected by what happens in
        it
Speaking of such a context
        is sometimes like presenting an
        egg but more like producing
        a bug—a bug continuing
        among bugs
I speak of sex strictly
        between ...
The heat but the drought
        of summer—everything only a
        moment of priority
And the propriety of the
        mouth with thought in it   *July 17, 1988*

181

The exhalation should or shouldn't
     count
Should
A sentence and ice
The dreams are almost silent
Something stimulated appetite
So someone feels more ample
     than usual taking up more
     space and time
An animal burned by cold
     is approaching from the right
     and there is no way
     to move so that it
     approaches from the left
Citizens are milling in the
     public grammar
Simple thirst and the related
     love of intoxication become examples
     of mute sentiments mutually held
     —because we didn't know what
     to say
Time is a mock function
     of the ocean
And a memory occurs in
     English
Calves
The animal looks like a
     cloud opposed to the wind
But all my judgments are
     threaded
I don't think I'd know

x, f, t, or any
one of my friends if
we encountered each other, me
as I am and he
or she naked with a
bag over his or her
head
Patricia?
Times change, up and down,
     in and out
Putting his hand through the
     shop window without breaking it,
     my father
Clearly I'd advocate an interpretation
     of dreams without etymology
But sexual redundancy—sexual things
     are encouraged
They can do
At the end of the
     bed, interpretable shoes
There are eyes in them
     therefore faces
The dark imploding
Almost all attributed
There are no unemployed noises,
     no noises without things
There is more noise than
     there are things

July 18, 1988

The dogs responded positively
Out of a single brain
Which they do

A big city dog is
        an urban rooster
Conservation, conservation!
The blindfolded horse is an
        owl and it's angry
The city ordinance that forbids
        the planting of poison oak

It's really not a dream
        but a description excited by
        particles
Wheel
White rain
"Already summer tilts its stringy
        shadows toward October"
The description which is convincing
        as the intervals
Otherwise words waste their length
And it will be as
        difficult to separate as to
        know the future
Verticalizing supine figures
In their sensitive state of
        perfection—with an interior mouth
        that speaks at this moment

      of someone—the skull replaces
      papers
Leaves fall ahead of their
      trees
A human dream in the
      attended bed, a human touch
Embraced by predictions
By conservations

August 3, 1988

My description is apprehensive
Then the genitals reached
That is the anti-narcissistic thought
        of it
A cough where peaches hang
The occasion didn't occur before
        this
The emotions in an area,
        the transmigration
The dream is passing through
        particles, between toes
But words are toes
But with hypotenuse
The mathematics of his or
        her monomania
286, 312
It's only an apparent problem,
        like tradition
This is voluntary poetry ... we
        are matrimonial people ... the poetry
        of volunteers
I was holding the child
        on my lap, reading to it
        to relieve anxiety
The buzz of the grasshoppers
        was very true, the mew
        of a bird
Lulled by dirty water hissed
        a pile driver and beside
        it stood its drivers

Dreams are superseded by suspense,
        suspense by society, society by
        anxiety
Anxiety is suspended
There's an ellipse to measure
        the true up and down,
        the verifiable (waking) in and
        out
The shift
Revolving, moving for enormity
For onlook, color

August 9, 1988

A beautiful sea of a
        chopped blue
With interruptions—but they are
        ovals
The sunlight in floating salts,
        wash, door, monopoly
That swells
There's no sardonic evidence for
        the kiss
For the man who formed
        a face with eyes awake
        it's I who am looking
        at this paper
The dream shakes but the
        real remains real
Am I awake?
I can't tell
How can I tell?
Well
If it seems to me
        that I am here and
        I really am here then
        I am awake
But am I here?
Something reminds me of the
        skin on a thistle but
        is thankful
A finger in a perception
        at the seashore
And the seashore without opposite

Elsewhere is there where yet
       an event has no effect
       while it tends toward one
The expression very carelessly like
       that of a passenger
The eyes covered (they covered
       an animal)
Aesthetic discoveries are themselves a
       theory made with belligerence
Blue

August 11, 1988

Are you a real mother?
But someone could ask this
        only if you were inconsistent
        with the mother you were
        before

There's too small a clock
        for the real intervals
Every night dreams incohere

But the doors are shut
        and the walls are romantically
        linked
Locations where the finger points
        and where the fingers cross

Lunch in a chair—lunching
        in a drone
But things plunge into description
        (words love their things)

And without promiscuity but in
        actual conversation
Drone and ant and dream

The many syllables in the
        emotional unit increase it
Describing, dream, and release it

                    August 13, 1988

The center floats between windows
The wind blows
Light forms myopia, revolving
It's all peripheral
The throttles of the light's
        referring

August 16, 1988

You might anticipate, to apprehend
Foreshortened sand
The sea is always disturbed
        —the edge in the thickness
        of thinking of it
Your flying ovals
It's hard to imagine anything
        more simple than dualism
To scale, sleep—are we
        not accurate?
A male accurate and a
        female accurate
You slept accidentally but I
        was awake and a great
        success of scale
There are dead in a
        cemetery to a degree
A person in Paris going
        to the end of the
        oval
A person in pants is
        not memory
A bird in pants is
        not realistic
A map
And I cast
I want the map with
        the greater history
A realization that comes too
        late for omission

Out of it things fell
     very close—no time
Throughout space confusion—memory, that
     separation from infinity

August 16, 1988

Familiarization is not good—it
      causes passion
She won't divert herself
Two beings end up with
      the words of which they
      are composed
Two beings end up
That thing must be pleasant
      —it lacks occasion for distractions
It is all proportions
The features are handsome and
      brave
The breasts are stubborn and
      observant
Every person is born preceded
      by its desire
Love finds something there and
      wants to be its modifier
Forehead, nose—profound as sleep
As retrospection
Let me tell you that
      she's pleased again—when worried
The face is lucky, fingers
      have their own body, the
      tongue another

August 21, 1988

194

Skies' blues break inverted in
            increments uppermost
The hand, palm in, automatically
            clings
Is it intelligence

A person in cold referring
            to the heart as a
            voluptuous hole
Whole blooms
Stillness in the hand as
            the brain knows despite some
            chipping at the constraints of
            perception

Poetry is not estimation
When I read this my
            head has been long
It can't go on forever

It has a neck and
            stomach (it should eat)
There is no marginality in
            metonymy
One speaks from a foregrounded
            eye, going from head

Head
Egg
Money

I have no objection to
        visibility
The holes into which a
        tree lusts in vertical holding
        descriptive floating clicks in leaf
Desire is a visual historian

August 27, 1988

Such is that which when
        we organize with reason we
        socialize
We separate
When I hear the word
        "method" I don't think of
        the activity "pencil-sharpening"
Distance
Animals are looking at you
A lamp with two necks
        of equal length to hold
        the head
A box of disks maybe
        too warm in the light
A bear in beautiful aestivation
No apple sings, no vanishing
        mechanics
Ourselves approaching the middle of
        the alphabet
My permanent mother was in
        her canoe when the heron
        was reflected
Time zigzagging an exciting unlived
        but experienced lifetime in anticipation
        patiently over July twenty-five
A dream disrupts verbalization
I too often write the
        article meaning to
There is only dependency if
        there's no background
Only metonymy (me, you)

Nakedness, then, is a form
     of honor
The delicate original is decisive
It is divided in its
     rhyme

August 30, 1988

Something crawls though the window
        in the night politically
I am discerning an enormous
        formal problem
An epic
It is very formal and
        falls as if on feet
Defeating the situation in a
        fortress consciousness
Brick is pale and the
        past is foreseeably disturbed
Can one know the world
        at any rate, a steady
        one
Colorless first, then a second
        yellow
Flicking the frocks of snails,
        beetles
Then a huge wave hits
        the beach at Santa Cruz
        and the sand fills its
        pocket
A pouch with two eyes
        or two clocks
The man should cook and
        on odd days
The dog carries its own
        weight in saddlebags
Gender is a motive—femininity,
        masculinity—its pleasure pressing in
        water

The window ripples the view
     through it of a wall,
     a wedge, a shopping cart
     pressed through mesh
The personality is not panoramic
Years in streaks and for
       years
Wars

September 2, 1988

There is pleasure in producing
        percussion, measure in intrusion
I like to let there
        be intrusion
A person is the host
        of her ears
The ears invert
And the eyes do
I like to let the
        eyes do
Colors dispersing sparkling asterisks
Curiosity anywhere overexposed
The person created its vulnerability
        in warm and cold air
        which attracts attention to attracting
        attention
Its question is looking backwards
The question is a plan
        —which plan?
Conjecture
Protection—that admirable consciousness
Your smile is your sand
It's beginning another pleasure in
        the middle of its message

September 11, 1988

My metonymic body part stands
     for solitude
It is a member of
     a standing society
Constantly
Like a jelly between two
     sticks, my subway line (well
     not completely mine) goes in
The person entering it is
     way out in its enmity
The person writing is way
     in in its attraction
But don't say "desire"—we
     should look rather for verification
Her first impression is of
     granules, grain, something yellow, a
     wasp, a lion, shades
Sleeplessness is a hazard of
     metonymy
So sleep is later deserving
     of intensity in spite of
     having to use the view
     finder for fear of losing
     the picture altogether
It being a bad habit
     to be tired
Like heating the area up
     so as to have open
     windows

I have a habit of mailing
        —with the social address of
        a metonymic mental part
An emotion of being a
        part

September 15, 1988

The emotions can be vandalized
Impossible to see
These emotions don't vault
We can sleep without distinction
        and without destination
The walls below the head
        when it thinks
Sleep, the war without prison
Every war is a sexual
        object
Every sight is a sexual
        objectification
But one represents a thing
        by its opposite
As it has hurt my
        eyes to select (such is
        the dispersive effect of description)
It appears like a jaundice
        in autumn
Scale
Animal
Into the proximity of
        violence admitted
No method submitted
Onions and rafts—ideas, dry
        land
To dream with mobility is
        almost impossible—knot by knot
        —to dream in achieving repetition

November 3 & 11, 1988

A noise of vicissitudes, of
        a remarked gully
It is rolling but not
        with speed
I am writing—which takes
        the observer's opacity
The room in a cliff
        in a coast on the
        city
The difference is a sequence
        of successive perceptions
Big dog's and little dog's
        efforts
I couldn't know whether or
        not to attribute to the
        animals an awareness of their
        own performance
But it offers contemporary women
        visual pleasure
And it is maintaining decomposition
        (which is sex)
Sand or sound
Writing is this unsystematized accumulation
        of statements and findings
Poles for the birds
That of which it is
        said it is rain
A silent voice sinking high

                            November 14, 1988

The commencement of meteorology is
        in plenitude not history
Nature is consequence
Midhead
And thrown out in life
        allotted a reality (for which
        I speak only of myself)
The wearer's weight walking in
        mud
Then weather, then libido
The middle and its sublimity
The bigness and brightness of
        a lull

November 14, 1988

From under the cape of
        penmanship the person signs its
        name
It is not it
Today the daylight is a
        marsh and the clouds squat
Such active and adequate activities
        without clairvoyant capacity
Which is a kind of
        literacy
The accurate droning in perspective,
        in ladder
Overlapping when the eyes are
        clear—events never pass enough
But all of persons have
        events
Waves are an itch and
        a manipulation
The churning of the clock
        on which seagulls float
It all comes back
A person exits a vagina
To reflect
Unconsciously grasses are worries
My dream was a consciously
        unconscious repetition
Pressing the brow of the
        bowl of the hand against
        some corrugations, some mockery
Its rungs to turn differently

November 18, 1988

Firefighters—conventional devices—passing in
        a hurry, the whole sky
        wet
The entire green
To read it requires a
        magnifying glass from the *OED*
Words organized and more than
        likely
Not looking at the homeless
        person to whom I've given
        money
Not asking him to know
        me in addition to taking
        money
Though I loved the music
        only a minute ago but
        was now irritated by it
Getting out of the chair
        again to set things just
        right where a corner of
        the carpet was folded under
A piece of paper on
        the floor—and yet this
        attention in no way lessens
The momentum of the practical
        helps
Echo
The manic concavity
Time in a spray and
        the person bare

I'd a spoon in my
        right hand with which I
        was making impressions
Time has the last word
        and explains nothing

November 18, 1988

Seeing as if seeing were
        solid in itself, and repeatedly
        recent
So I look back in
        the outskirts
In water—there's no immunity
        from motes
As train tracks come naturally
        from a trajectory a person
        can stay still
She (or he) gets mildly
        ill with little commotion
Minutes shutter
There's no opposite—it's not
        imperfect to mediate
Or with a pencil—that
        lengthening, fading young stubble
Of a whole landscape there
        is a rock to be
        seen
He, as one can see
One is a metonymic production
        of natural history quivering
Remaining in my lessons at
        this rate always more intimate
But quivering is an example
        of permeable intonations
The banging of a train
Pedagogical memories

This must be it
Memory is the present faintly
        motivated

November 19, 1988

Inert wind through the trees
     and rain working wet on
     wet
In guilt one betrays philosophy
Good but random coincidences held
     my curiosity on the first
     40 years
The action of brown birds
I don't know that this
     winter is beginning earlier and
     wetter than before
It matters however exactly as
     a book
It's in a satisfaction—the
     content of a satisfaction
A sexual one who remembers
     the wall
There are so many metonyms,
     none dim
But they are the opposite
     of qualities—yet there are
     no opposites
Recently someone credited me with
     saying that writing sees
But I never meant it
Writing the eyeing which is
     that of a person's
The pack which it is
     for it to remember

Beyond compare—so there's something
        sexual
Then something gradual

November 22, 1988

All sentences about the sense
        of seeing, the sense of
        embarrassment
It could all disappear—instead
        it appeared
My language
My language is a genital—
        let's say that
My language, in part
Thinking is *like* the composition
        of things
Distinctions steering sunlight
A field of horses is
        a landmark but not a
        particular horse stirring in the
        terrain
Knuckles, or knocking from a
        train
A thirst produced by onion
You cannot concentrate on oblivion
The eye applies a visage
        to the cloud
No thought of rain tonight
        though clouds of provenance
How to write
There is bas-relief
I see Marcus Aurelius and
        a water buffalo
"Your American feminism is suggesting
        women's sex," he said
It could all disappear

Streets
With remorse for individualism, provoking
     scale
Dimension sinks
It's the event of seeing
     what I speak of with
     someone's eyes
The event of a carnality
     covered by eye
The light proceeding along the
     yellow sides of night
A word is a panorama
     of a thing
It's the eye's duty to
     tell
It's relevant—though a person
     is implicated in the process
     it keeps in sight

November 23, 29,
& December 1, 1988

A person's character is in
         the realm of possibility
This means hysteria
Someone, probably I, says "It
         isn't your feet it's your
         shoes"
This is meant to be
         comforting
For one moment this too
         means hysteria but without loss
         of the lively consciousness of
         personality
The single brain of self
         and many examples
The diameter of a rain
         drop one-sixth the diameter of
         the splash it makes on
         the street
The verified impression of a
         friendliness as oblique
A person appearing does not
         undertake its introspection except at
         the appearance of its appearance
But why arrive at Fahrenheit
         and so little resemblance
There is very little melancholy
         between a thing and a
         word that presents it
Whatever the mind tends to
         suppose, there is psychological or
         morphological attachment to it

Might it come to the
      consciousness of unconsciousness
It is good to know
      so

January 21, 1989

LYN HEJINIAN

Born in the San Francisco bay area in 1941, Lyn Hejinian graduated from Harvard University in 1963.

She began writing poetry as early as grammar school, and began publishing her first works in magazines in 1963 and 1964. By the mid 1970s she had begun editing her distinguished Tuumba Press series, which included a wide range of contemporary poetry, including works by many of the San Francisco and New York City acquaintances which soon would join forces in the social, political, and aesthetic grouping of the "Language" poets in the Bay area.

In 1976 she published *A Thought Is the Bride of What Thinking*, following it over the next two years with *A Mask of Motion* and the now underground poetry "classic," *Gesauldo*. This work combined lyrical poetry with a narrative structure set across brief phrases or "titles," which poetically grounded the longer narrative-like passages, a device she would use later in *My Life*.

Gesauldo brought her further national attention, and later that same year the noted poetry publisher Geoff Young printed her first major work of poetry, *Writing Is an Aid to Memory*. In this work Hejinian began laying out her notions of the relationship of writing and memory along the lines of the ideas expressed earlier in the century by Gertrude Stein. For Hejinian, conscious always of what she calls "the disquieting runs of life slipping by," knowledge is not a complete thing, but is "part of the whole...from which love seeks to contrast knowledge with separation, and certainty with the temporal." For Hejinian writing itself—an act that is simultaneously one of forgetting and remembering—is a definition or an "aid" to redefinition of the past.

In *My Life* Hejinian further explored her own past and autobiography. Writing it in 1978, in her 37th year, Hejinian constructed a work of 37 sections of 37 sentences, each section paralleling the year of her life. For the second Sun & Moon edition, published eight years later, Hejinian added 8 sections and 8 new sentences to each previous section to account for her current age.

Upon its first publication in 1980 *My Life* acheived international acclaim and quickly sold out. The second edition is now in its third printing and is taught in high schools, colleges, and universities throughout the United States and Canada.

In 1983 Hejinian joined her husband, the jazz saxophonist Larry Ochs, on a tour with ROVA Saxophone Quartet to Leningrad and Moscow. While in the Soviet Union Hejinian met several contemporary poets, including the Leningrad experimentalist, Arkadii Dragomoschenko. In the years following she corresponded extensively with Dragomoschenko, teaching him English and herself Russian in the process. The result of this intimate correspondence was a translation of Dragomoschenko's *Description* (Sun & Moon Classic: 9) and the interchange between a great number of contemporary American and Soviet poets. Most recently, she collaborated with Michael Davidson, Ron Silliman, and Barrett Watten on a book-length work, *Leningrad*. And she is currently at work on translating another collection of Dragomoschenko's poetry.

Hejinian's other books include *Redo* and *The Guard*, both published in 1984.

SUN & MOON CLASSICS

Sun & Moon Classics is a publicly supported nonprofit program to publish new editions and translations or republications of outstanding world literature of the late-nineteenth and twentieth centuries. Organized by the Contemporary Arts Educational Project, Inc., a non-profit corporation, and published by its program, Sun & Moon Press, the series is made possible, in part, by grants and individual contributions.

This book was made possible, in part, through a matching grant from the California Arts Council, the Cultural Affairs Department of the City of Los Angeles, the Andrew W. Mellon Foundation, and through contributions from the following individuals:

Charles Altieri (Seattle, Washington)
John Arden (Galway, Ireland)
Dennis Barone (West Harford, Connecticut)
Jonathan Baumbach (Brooklyn, New York)
Steve Benson (Berkeley, California)
Sherry Bernstein (New York, New York)
Robert Crosson (Los Angeles, California)
Tina Darragh and P. Inman (Greenbelt, Maryland)
Fielding Dawson (New York, New York)
Christopher Dewdney (Toronto, Canada)
Philip Dunne (Malibu, California)
George Economou (Norman, Oklahoma)
Elaine Equi and Jerome Sala (New York, New York)
Richard Foreman (New York, New York)
Howard N. Fox (Los Angeles, California)
Jerry Fox (Aventura, Florida)
In Memoriam: Rose Fox
Melvyn Freilicher (San Diego, California)
Peter Glassgold (Brooklyn, New York)
Fred Haines (Los Angeles, California)
Fanny Howe (La Jolla, California)
Harold Jaffe (San Diego, California)
Ira S. Jaffe (Albuquerque, New Mexico)
Perla and Amiram V. Karney (Bel Air, California)
Alex Katz (New York, New York)
Herbert Lust (Greenwich, Connecticut)
Norman MacAffee (new York, New York)
Rosemary Macchiavelli (Washington, D.C.)
In Memoriam: John Mandanis
Maggie O'Sullivan (Hebben Bridge, England)
Rochelle Owens (Norman, Oklahoma)

SUN & MOON CLASSICS

DATE DUE